Dedication

This book is dedicated to my two sons Omari and Beracah who I call my miracle babies because I had them after struggling with infertility.

Inside Jack's little mouth, lived 20 white sparkly baby teeth.

Jack loved eating sweets too much.

This was not very good for his 20 sparkly teeth because little **germs** would come and climb up the teeth.

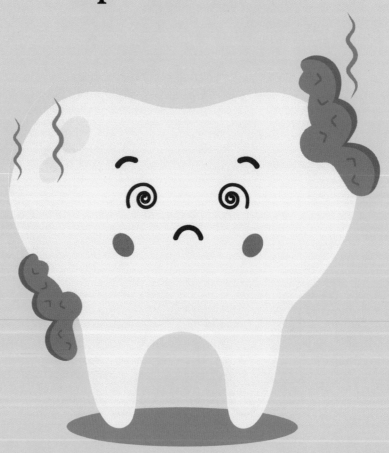

The germs would get very excited and enjoy the sweets too.

Whenever Jack **stopped** eating sweets the germs got really sad, hungry and would cry; then demand for more sweets.

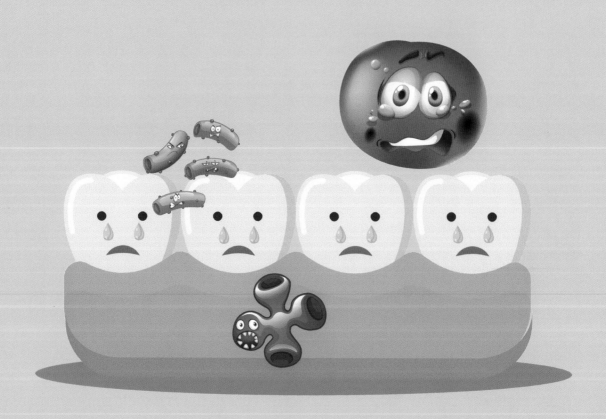

Because Jack had a sweet tooth, he kept on eating more and more sweet snacks.

Then the germs created little black and brown holes on the 20 sparkly teeth

They started looking grimy, yucky and spotty

The 20 sparkly teeth started hurting.

This made Jack
cry and cry and cry

Jack went to his Mum for a **cuddle** showing her where it hurts.

When Jack's Mum saw the black and brown holes, she was so shocked!

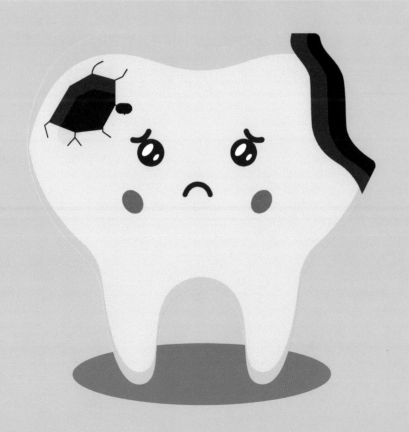

The next morning she called the **dentist** for help

Jack was asked to go to the dentist as soon as possible

Jack and his Mum hopped on the **bus** and went to the dentist

The dentist was **happy** to see Jack

She **repaired** the brown and black holes

Then the dentist politely asked Jack to **stop eating too many sweets,**

Brush his teeth twice a day to keep the germs away, which he did.

Jack was given a sticker for being brave.

And he was happy ever after.

THE END

Printed in Great Britain
by Amazon

77949452R00016